Bead Jewelry Making For Beginners

A Step-by-Step Guide to Creating
Beautiful Beaded Jewelry

Copyright@2023

Cashel Memphis

Table Of Content

Chapter 1: Introduction 4

Section 1- What Is Bead Jewelry Making?

....4

Section 2- Benefits Of Making Bead

Jewelry 6

Section 3- Basic Tools And Materials

Needed..8

Chapter 2: Types Of Beads 11

Section 1- Basic Overview Of Various

Types Of Beads 11

Section 2- Differences Between Seed

Beads, Glass Beads, Crystal Beads, And

More 19

Section 3- How To Choose The Right

Beads For Your Project 22

Chapter 3: Techniques For Bead Jewelry

Making 25

Section 1- Stringing Beads 25

Section 2- Using Crimp Beads 28

Section 3- Creating Wire Loops...........31

Section 4- Knotting 34

Section 5- Using Jump Rings 36

Chapter 4: Designing Your Bead Jewelry .39

Section 1- Choosing A Design 39

Section 2- Sketching Out Your Design 42

Section 3- Choosing Color Schemes 45

Section 4- Adding Embellishments 48

Chapter 5: Making Bead Jewelry Projects.51

Section 1- Earrings 52

Section 2- Bracelets 55

Section 3- Necklaces 58

Section 4- Anklets 61

Chapter 6: Troubleshooting And Tips 64

Section 1- Common Mistakes And Instructional Guide To Fix Them 64

Section 2- Tips For Creating Professional-Looking Jewelry 67

Chapter 7: Selling Your Bead Jewelry 72

Section 1- Tips For Selling Your Bead Jewelry 72

Section 2- Setting Up An Online Store 75

Section 3- Marketing Your Jewelry 78

Chapter 8: Conclusion.............................81

Section 1- Summary Of Key Points.....81

Section 2- Inspiration For Future Bead

Jewelry Projects 84

Section 3- Final Thoughts And

Encouragement For Continuing To

Create Beautiful Bead Jewelry.............87

Chapter 1: Introduction

Section 1- What Is Bead Jewelry Making?

Bead jewelry making is a form of jewelry making that involves using beads to create necklaces, bracelets, earrings, and other types of jewelry. Beads come in a variety of materials, shapes, sizes, and colors, such as glass, crystal, seed, and wood. The art of bead jewelry making involves stringing and arranging beads in a specific pattern or design to create unique and beautiful pieces of jewelry. This craft is popular among beginners and experienced jewelry makers alike, as it allows for a wide range of creativity and personalization.

Section 2- Benefits Of Making Bead Jewelry

There are several benefits to making bead jewelry, including:

1. Creative expression: Making bead jewelry allows you to express your creativity and individuality by creating unique pieces that reflect your personal style and taste.

2. Relaxation and stress relief: The repetitive motions of beading can be meditative and soothing, providing a way to relieve stress and anxiety.

3. Cost-effective: Making bead jewelry can be a cost-effective alternative to buying expensive pieces of jewelry. By purchasing beads and other materials in bulk, you can create multiple pieces of jewelry for a fraction of the cost.

4. Personalized gifts: Bead jewelry makes great gifts for friends and family. By creating custom pieces, you can give a gift that is both thoughtful and unique.

5. Social activity: Bead jewelry making can be a social activity, allowing you to connect with others who share your interest in jewelry making. You can also join online forums and groups to share ideas and tips with others.

6. Business opportunities: If you develop a passion for bead jewelry making, it can also lead to business opportunities. You can sell your creations at craft fairs, online marketplaces, or even start your own jewelry-making business.

Section 3- Basic Tools And Materials Needed

Here are some basic tools and materials needed for bead jewelry making:

1. Beads: The most important material for bead jewelry making is, of course, beads. There are many different types of beads available, such as glass, crystal, plastic, wood, and more. Choose the type of beads that you like best and that are suitable for your project.

2. Jewelry wire: Jewelry wire is used to string and connect the beads together. There are several different types of wire, such as beading wire, memory wire, and craft wire. Beading wire is the most commonly used wire for bead jewelry making.

3. Jewelry pliers: Pliers are essential tools for bead jewelry making. Round-nose pliers are used to create loops and curves in wire, while flat-nose pliers are used to hold and manipulate wire.

4. Crimp beads: Crimp beads are used to secure the ends of beading wire and prevent the beads from falling off.

5. Clasps: Clasps are used to fasten the jewelry around the neck or wrist. There are many different types of clasps available, such as lobster clasps, spring-ring clasps, and toggle clasps.

6. Jump rings: Jump rings are small metal rings used to connect different parts of the jewelry together.

7. Beading mat: A beading mat is a soft surface used to prevent beads from rolling around and getting lost.

8. Scissors: Scissors are used to cut wire and string.

9. Beading needle: A beading needle is a thin needle used to help string beads onto wire.

These are the basic tools and materials needed to start making bead jewelry. As you progress and become more experienced, you may find that you need additional tools and materials for more advanced projects.

Chapter 2: Types Of Beads

Section 1- Basic Overview Of Various Types Of Beads

There are many different types of beads available for bead jewelry making. Below is a significant overview of some of the most typical and common types:

1. Seed Beads:

Seed beads are small, uniform beads that are often used for bead weaving and embroidery.

They come in a variety of sizes, ranging from very small (15/0) to larger (6/0), and are available in a wide range of colors.

2. Glass Beads:

Glass beads are made of glass and come in a variety of shapes, sizes, and colors. They can be smooth or faceted, and can be transparent, opaque, or translucent.

3. Crystal Beads:

Crystal beads are made of leaded glass and have a high level of clarity and sparkle. They come in a variety of shapes and sizes and are often used for more formal or elegant jewelry.

4. Gemstone Beads:

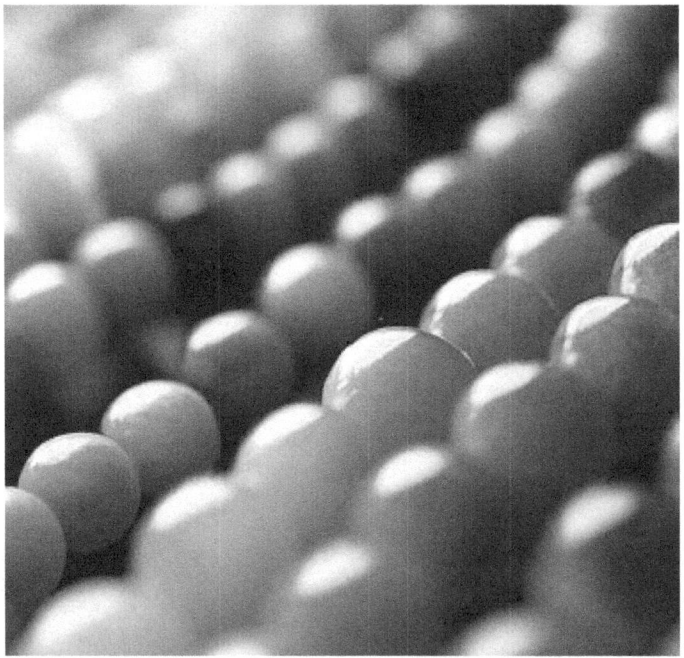

Gemstone beads are made from natural stones such as amethyst, jade, turquoise, and many others. They come in a variety of colors and shapes and can add a unique and natural element to your jewelry.

5. Acrylic Beads:

Acrylic beads are lightweight and come in a variety of shapes and colors. They are often used for larger or more bold jewelry pieces.

6. Metal Beads:

Metal beads are made of various types of metal, such as sterling silver, copper, brass, or pewter. They can be smooth or textured, and can add a unique element to your jewelry.

7. Wooden Beads:

Wooden beads are made of various types of wood and come in a variety of shapes and sizes. They can be natural or painted, and add a warm and natural element to your jewelry.

These are just a few of the many different types of beads available for bead jewelry making. Experiment with different types of beads to find the ones that work best for your projects and personal style.

Section 2- Differences Between Seed Beads, Glass Beads, Crystal Beads, And More

Seed beads, glass beads, crystal beads, and gemstone beads are some of the most popular types of beads used in jewelry making. Below are a number of the main as well as significant differences between them:

1. Seed beads: Seed beads are small, round beads that come in a variety of sizes and colors. They are often used in bead weaving and embroidery, and are typically sold in hanks or strands. Seed beads are usually made of glass, but can also be made of other materials such as metal, plastic, or clay.

2. Glass beads: Glass beads are made of glass and come in a wide variety of shapes, sizes, and colors. They can be smooth or faceted, and can be transparent, opaque, or translucent. Glass beads are popular for all types of jewelry making, and are often used for more affordable or casual pieces.

3. Crystal beads: Crystal beads are made of leaded glass and have a high level of clarity and sparkle. They come in a variety of shapes and sizes and are often used for more formal or elegant jewelry. Swarovski crystal beads are a popular brand of crystal beads used in jewelry making.

4. Gemstone beads: Gemstone beads are made from natural stones such as amethyst, jade, turquoise, and many others. They come in a variety of colors and shapes and can add a unique and natural element to your jewelry. Gemstone beads can be more expensive than other types of beads, but can add significant value to your jewelry.

5. Metal beads: Metal beads are made of various types of metal, such as sterling silver, copper, brass, or pewter. They can be smooth or textured, and can add a unique element to your jewelry. Metal beads can be more expensive than other types of beads, but can also add significant value to your jewelry.

Overall, the choice of bead depends on the type of jewelry you want to create and the effect you want to achieve. Experimenting with different types of beads can help you discover your personal style and preferences.

Section 3- How To Choose The Right Beads For Your Project

Choosing the right beads for your project can depend on a variety of factors such as the type of jewelry you are making, the style you want to achieve, and the skill level required for the project. Here are some tips to help you choose the right beads for your project:

1. Consider the type of jewelry: Different types of jewelry require different types of beads. For example, seed beads are commonly used for bead weaving, while gemstone beads are often used for making beaded bracelets and necklaces. Consider the type of jewelry you want to make and choose beads that are suitable for that project.

2. Think about color: The color of the beads you choose can have a big impact on the final look of your jewelry. Consider the color scheme you want to use and choose beads that complement or contrast with the other materials you are using.

3. Consider size: Beads come in a wide range of sizes, from tiny seed beads to larger gemstone beads. The size of the beads you choose can affect the overall look of your jewelry. For example, larger beads may be more suitable for making statement pieces, while smaller beads may be better for delicate or intricate designs.

4. Consider shape and texture: Beads come in a variety of shapes and textures, including round, square, faceted, smooth, and more. Think about the style of jewelry you want to create and choose beads that fit that style.

5. Experiment: Don't be afraid to experiment with different types of beads to find the ones that work best for your project. Try mixing different types of beads together or using unconventional materials to create unique and one-of-a-kind pieces.

By considering these factors and experimenting with different types of beads, you can choose the right beads for your project and create beautiful and personalized jewelry.

Chapter 3: Techniques For Bead Jewelry Making

Section 1- Stringing Beads

Stringing beads is one of the most basic and essential techniques in jewelry making. Below are a number essential steps to follow when stringing beads:

1. Choose your stringing material: There are several types of stringing materials to choose from, including nylon thread, silk cord, beading wire, and more. Choose a stringing material that is strong enough to hold the weight of your beads, but also thin enough to fit through the holes.

2. Cut your stringing material to the desired length: Use a pair of scissors to cut your stringing material to the desired length, leaving some extra length for tying knots and attaching a clasp.

3. Thread your beads onto the string: Slide your beads onto the stringing material, one at a time. Use a bead stopper or a piece of tape to keep the beads from falling off the other end of the string.

4. Tie a knot: After you have strung all your beads, tie a knot at the end of the string to keep the beads from sliding off. You can also add a bead tip or a crimp bead to secure the end of the string.

5. Add a clasp: If you are making a bracelet or necklace, you will need to add a clasp to the end of the string. Use jump rings or bead caps to attach the clasp to the string.

6. Finish your piece: Once you have added the clasp, trim any excess stringing material and add a dab of glue to the knots or crimp beads to keep them from coming undone.

By following these steps, you can easily string beads and create beautiful and personalized jewelry.

Section 2- Using Crimp Beads

Crimp beads are small metal beads used to secure the ends of beading wire or stringing material. Here's how to use crimp beads in your jewelry making projects:

1. Cut your beading wire or stringing material to the desired length, leaving some extra length for attaching a clasp.

2. Thread a crimp bead onto the wire or stringing material.

3. Thread the wire or stringing material through the loop of the clasp, then back through the crimp bead. Make sure the wire or stringing material is straight and there are no kinks or twists.

4. Use crimping pliers to flatten the crimp bead. Position the crimp bead in the larger crimping notch of the pliers, then gently squeeze the pliers to flatten the bead. This will secure the wire or stringing material in place.

5. Trim any excess wire or stringing material.

6. Add a crimp cover (optional). If you want to hide the crimp bead, you can use a crimp cover. Thread the crimp cover onto the wire

or stringing material, then use flat nose pliers to gently close the cover over the crimp bead.

By using crimp beads, you can create secure and professional-looking finishes for your jewelry projects. It may take some practice to master crimping, but once you get the hang of it, you'll be able to create beautiful and sturdy jewelry pieces.

Section 3- Creating Wire Loops

Wire loops are an essential component in jewelry making and are used to connect beads and findings together. Below are a number of the steps to create a basic wire loop:

1. Cut a piece of wire to the desired length using wire cutters. The length of wire you need will depend on your project, but it's better to cut a little extra than not enough.

2. Grip the end of the wire with round nose pliers, about 1-2cm from the end of the wire.

3. Use your thumb or finger to bend the wire over the top of the pliers, creating a small loop.

4. Reposition the pliers so that they are in the loop, with the bottom jaw of the pliers inside the loop.

5. Use your fingers or chain nose pliers to grip the end of the wire and wrap it around the base of the loop, making sure the wire is tight against the base of the loop and there are no gaps.

6. Use wire cutters to trim any excess wire, leaving a small tail.

7. Use chain nose pliers to gently squeeze the end of the wire tail against the base of the loop, so that it blends in with the rest of the loop.

8. Repeat steps 2-7 to create additional wire loops as needed.

By following these steps, you can create secure and professional-looking wire loops for your jewelry projects. With practice, you can experiment with different sizes and shapes of wire loops to add variety to your designs.

Section 4- Knotting

Knotting is a technique used in jewelry making to create a secure and decorative finish for bracelets and necklaces. Here's how to knot beads for jewelry making:

1. Cut a length of beading cord to the desired length. Make sure to add a few extra inches to account for knotting and attaching a clasp.

2. Thread a knotting bead onto the beading cord, then tie a knot at the end of the cord to keep the bead from falling off.

3. Thread a bead onto the cord, then tie a knot on the other side of the bead. Make sure the knot is tight against the bead, but not so tight that it distorts the shape of the bead.

4. Repeat step 3, adding beads and knots one at a time until you have reached the desired length.

5. To finish, thread a knotting bead onto the cord, then tie a knot at the end of the cord to keep the bead in place.

6. Add a clasp or jump ring to the ends of the cord to create a finished bracelet or necklace.

When knotting beads, it's important to make sure the knots are tight and evenly spaced to create a professional-looking finish. It may take some practice to get the hang of knotting, but once you master the technique, you can create beautiful and durable jewelry pieces.

Section 5- Using Jump Rings

Jump rings are small metal rings used to connect different components of a jewelry piece, such as clasps, pendants, and beads. Here's how to use jump rings in your jewelry making projects:

1. Open the jump ring using two pairs of pliers. Hold one side of the jump ring with one pair of pliers and hold the other side of

the jump ring with the other pair of pliers. Twist one pair of pliers towards you and the other pair away from you to open the jump ring. Avoid pulling the jump ring apart by pulling both ends away from each other, as this will weaken the ring and make it harder to close properly.

2. Thread the open jump ring through the component you want to attach, such as a clasp or a pendant.

3. Thread the jump ring through the component you want to connect it to, such as a bead or another jump ring.

4. Use the pliers to close the jump ring, making sure the ends meet and there are no gaps. Make sure you twist the jump ring back into its original shape and avoid bending it out of shape, as this could weaken the ring and make it easier to break.

5. Repeat steps 1-4 to add additional jump rings as needed.

By using jump rings, you can create secure and versatile connections between different components of your jewelry projects. With practice, you can experiment with different sizes and shapes of jump rings to add variety to your designs.

Chapter 4: Designing Your Bead Jewelry

Section 1- Choosing A Design

Choosing a design for your bead jewelry project can be a fun and creative process. Below are some vital tips to help you choose a design:

1. Consider your skill level: If you are a beginner, start with simple designs that use basic techniques like stringing beads or making wire loops. As you gain more experience, you can move on to more complex designs that involve more advanced techniques.

2. Think about the occasion: Consider the occasion or purpose of the jewelry piece you are making. Is it for everyday wear or a special event? The occasion can help guide the design and materials you choose.

3. Look for inspiration: Browse through jewelry making magazines, and websites for inspiration. You can also look at finished jewelry pieces or beading supplies at a craft store for ideas.

4. Choose a color scheme: Choose a color scheme that complements your personal style or the occasion for which the jewelry piece will be worn. Consider the color of the beads, findings, and wire you use in your design.

5. Experiment with different bead sizes and shapes: Different bead sizes and shapes can add variety and interest to your design. Try mixing and matching beads to create a unique and eye-catching look.

6. Sketch your design: Sketch out your design before you start making the jewelry piece. This can help you visualize the final product and make adjustments to the design as needed.

Keep in mind that there are basically no rules while creating jewelry. Try new things and explore without fear. The most important thing is to have fun and enjoy the process of creating something beautiful and unique.

Section 2- Sketching Out Your Design

Sketching out your design before you start making your bead jewelry piece can help you visualize the final product and make adjustments as needed. Here are some tips for sketching out your design:

1. Use a pencil: Start by using a pencil to sketch out your design. This will allow you to make changes or adjustments as you go.

2. Choose the right paper: Use a blank sheet of paper or a sketchbook to draw your design. Make sure the paper is large enough to accommodate the size of your jewelry piece.

3. Consider the proportions: When sketching your design, pay attention to the proportions of the beads and other components. Make sure they are balanced and visually appealing.

4. Label the components: Label each component of your design, such as the clasp, beads, and findings. This will help you keep track of what you need and where each component should be placed.

5. Add details: Add details to your sketch, such as the color and size of each bead, the type of wire or stringing material you will use, and any decorative elements or charms you plan to add.

6. Make changes as needed: If you notice any issues or design flaws while sketching, make changes to your design.

Remember, your sketch does not have to be perfect or exact. It's simply a tool to help you plan out your design and ensure that you have all the necessary components and materials before you start making your jewelry piece.

Section 3- Choosing Color Schemes

Choosing a color scheme is an important aspect of designing bead jewelry. Here are some tips to help you choose the right color scheme for your project:

1. Consider the occasion: The occasion for which the jewelry piece will be worn can help guide your color choices. For example, if it's a formal event, you may want to choose colors that are more subdued, while for a fun and casual event, you may want to choose brighter colors.

2. Look for inspiration: Look for inspiration in your surroundings, such as the colors of nature, art, or fashion. You can also browse through magazines, websites, and social media platforms for color ideas.

3. Use the color wheel: The color wheel can be a helpful tool to choose complementary colors. Complementary hues, such as blue and orange or red and green, are opposite each other on the color wheel. These colors can create a harmonious and balanced color scheme.

4. Choose a monochromatic color scheme: A monochromatic color scheme involves using different shades and tones of a single color. This can create a sophisticated and elegant look.

5. Use contrasting colors: Contrasting colors, such as black and white, or red and green, can create a bold and striking color scheme. Be careful not to use too many contrasting colors, as it can be overwhelming.

6. Consider skin tone: The skin tone of the person who will be wearing the jewelry can also influence the color choices. For example, warmer tones can complement skin with warm undertones, while cooler tones can complement skin with cool undertones.

Keep in mind, there are no sticky and quick rules when it comes to selecting color schemes. The most important thing is to choose colors that you love and that complement your personal style and the occasion for which the jewelry piece will be worn.

Section 4- Adding Embellishments

Adding embellishments to your bead jewelry piece can give it a unique and personalized touch. Here are some popular embellishments you can use:

1. Charms: Charms can be attached to your jewelry piece using jump rings or wire. They come in a variety of shapes, sizes, and materials, such as metal, enamel, and glass.

2. Pendants: Pendants can be used as a focal point for your jewelry piece. They can be attached using jump rings or wire and can be made of various materials, such as metal, gemstones, or glass.

3. Tassels: Tassels can add movement and texture to your jewelry piece. They can be made of various materials, such as silk, cotton, or leather.

4. Ribbons and cords: Ribbons and cords can be used to create a unique look for your jewelry piece. They can be used to tie or wrap around beads, or to create a necklace or bracelet.

5. Bead caps: Bead caps can be used to add a decorative touch to your beads. They come in various sizes and materials, such as metal, filigree, or rhinestone.

6. Rhinestones: Rhinestones can be added to your jewelry piece to add a sparkly touch. They can be attached using glue or wire.

When adding embellishments, it's important to consider the overall design of your jewelry piece. Make sure the embellishments complement the colors and materials you've already chosen and don't overwhelm the design.

Chapter 5: Making Bead Jewelry Projects

Step-by-step instructions for creating simple bead jewelry projects:

Section 1- Earrings

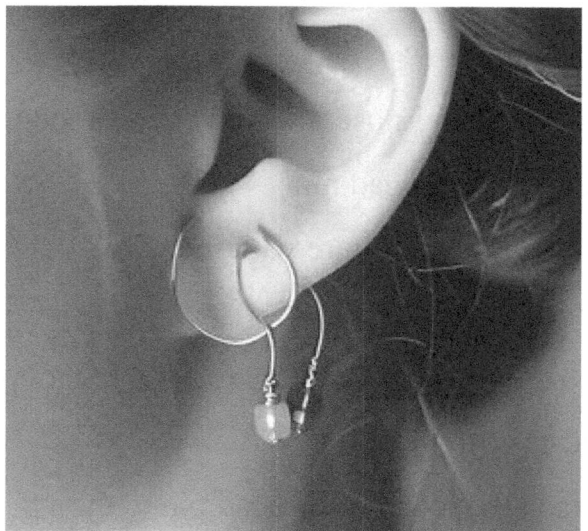

Making earrings can be a fun and easy way to start making bead jewelry. Here are the steps to make a simple pair of bead earrings:

Materials:

- Two ear wires
- Two head pins
- Any choice of two beads
- Round-nose pliers
- Wire cutters

Steps:

1. Choose your beads and slide them onto the head pins.

2. Use the round-nose pliers to create a loop at the top of the head pin.

3. Trim any excess wire with the wire cutters.

4. Use the round-nose pliers to open the loop on the ear wire.

5. Attach the loop on the head pin to the loop on the ear wire.

6. Close the loop on the ear wire using the round-nose pliers.

7. You should repeat the process in order to create a second earring.

Tips:

- You can use different types of beads, such as glass, crystal, or seed beads, to create different looks.

- Experiment with different earring findings, such as hoop earrings or clip-on earrings.
- Add embellishments, such as charms or tassels, to create a more personalized look.

Remember to have fun and be creative when 1making earrings. They are a great way to showcase your personal style and add a pop of color to any outfit.

Section 2- Bracelets

Making bracelets is a great way to express your personal style and create a unique accessory to wear. Here are the steps to make a simple beaded bracelet:

Materials:
- Beads of your choice
- Beading wire
- Crimp beads

- Clasp
- Crimping pliers
- Wire cutters

Steps:

1. Choose your beads and string them onto the beading wire.

2. Measure the length of the beading wire to fit your wrist, leaving a little extra for the clasp and crimp beads.

3. Slide a crimp bead onto one end of the wire, followed by the clasp.

4. Loop the wire back through the crimp bead, and use the crimping pliers to crimp the bead.

5. Trim any excess wire with the wire cutters.

6. String your beads onto the wire, leaving a little extra space at the end for the second crimp bead and clasp.

7. Slide a crimp bead onto the end of the wire, followed by the clasp.

8. Loop the wire back through the crimp bead, and use the crimping pliers to crimp the bead.

9. Trim any excess wire with the wire cutters.

Tips:

- You can experiment with different bead patterns, colors, and sizes to create unique designs.

- Use different types of clasps, such as toggle or magnetic clasps, to add variety to your bracelets.

- Add charms or other embellishments to create a personalized touch.

Remember to have fun and be creative when making bracelets. They are a great accessory to wear alone or stack with other bracelets to create a layered look.

Section 3- Necklaces

Making necklaces can be a bit more involved than making earrings or bracelets, but the process can still be enjoyable and rewarding. Here are the steps to make a simple beaded necklace:

Materials:

- Beads of your choice
- Beading wire
- Crimp beads

- Clasp

- Crimping pliers

- Wire cutters

Steps:

1. Choose your beads and string them onto the beading wire in your desired pattern.

2. Measure the length of the beading wire to fit your neck, leaving a little extra for the clasp and crimp beads.

3. Slide a crimp bead onto one end of the wire, followed by the clasp.

4. Loop the wire back through the crimp bead, and use the crimping pliers to crimp the bead.

5. Trim any excess wire with the wire cutters.

6. String your beads onto the wire, leaving a little extra space at the end for the second crimp bead and clasp.

7. Slide a crimp bead onto the end of the wire, followed by the clasp.

8. Loop the wire back through the crimp bead, and use the crimping pliers to crimp the bead.

9. Trim any excess wire with the wire cutters.

Tips:

- You can use different types of beads and mix them together to create unique designs.

- Experiment with different bead sizes and shapes to add dimension to your necklace.

- Use a variety of clasps, such as lobster claw or spring ring clasps, to add versatility to your necklace.

- Add a pendant or focal bead to create a statement piece.

Remember to have fun and be creative when making necklaces. They are a great way to showcase your personal style and add a touch of elegance to any outfit.

Section 4- Anklets

Anklets are a fun and easy jewelry project to make, and they can add a touch of bohemian flair to your outfit. Here are the steps to make a simple beaded anklet:

Materials:
- Beads of your choice
- Beading wire
- Crimp beads
- Clasp
- Crimping pliers

- Wire cutters

Steps:

1. Choose your beads and string them onto the beading wire in your desired pattern.

2. Measure the length of the beading wire to fit your ankle, leaving a little extra for the clasp and crimp beads.

3. Slide a crimp bead onto one end of the wire, followed by the clasp.

4. Loop the wire back through the crimp bead, and use the crimping pliers to crimp the bead.

5. Trim any excess wire with the wire cutters.

6. String your beads onto the wire, leaving a little extra space at the end for the second crimp bead and clasp.

7. Slide a crimp bead onto the end of the wire, followed by the clasp.

8. Loop the wire back through the crimp bead, and use the crimping pliers to crimp the bead.

9. Trim any excess wire with the wire cutters.

Tips:

- You can use a variety of bead sizes and colors to create a unique anklet.

- Experiment with different bead shapes and materials, such as shells or gemstones, to add texture and interest to your anklet.

- Use a charm or other embellishment to add a personal touch.

- Try layering anklets of different lengths and styles for a trendy look.

Remember to have fun and be creative when making anklets. They are a great way to showcase your personal style and add a playful touch to any outfit.

Chapter 6: Troubleshooting And Tips

Section 1- Common Mistakes And Instructional Guide To Fix Them

Here are some common mistakes that beginners may encounter when making bead jewelry and how to fix them:

1. Uneven or loose tension: This can result in a piece of jewelry that looks messy or falls apart easily. To fix this, try to keep an even tension as you bead and check your work periodically to ensure that it is snug.

2. Using the wrong type or size of wire: Choosing the wrong type or size of wire can cause problems such as kinking or breaking. To fix this, make sure to use a wire that is appropriate for your project and handle it gently to avoid damage.

3. Incorrect crimping: If your crimps are not holding or are too visible, this could be due to improper crimping. To fix this, make sure to use crimping pliers and follow the instructions carefully. Be sure to use the appropriate size crimp bead for your wire, and use enough tension to secure the wire in place.

4. Beads falling off or not sitting properly: This can be due to using a wire that is too thin or not stringing the beads tightly enough. To fix this, use a thicker wire or adjust your tension to ensure that the beads stay in place.

5. Using too many different bead types or colors: This can result in a piece that looks cluttered or unappealing. To fix this, try to choose a few complementary colors and bead types that work well together, and focus on creating a cohesive design.

Remember that making mistakes is a natural part of the learning process, and don't be discouraged if you encounter challenges along the way. With practice and patience, you can overcome these common mistakes and create beautiful, professional-looking bead jewelry.

Section 2- Tips For Creating Professional-Looking Jewelry

Here are some tips for creating professional-looking bead jewelry:

1. Use high-quality materials: Invest in quality beads, wire, and findings to ensure that your jewelry looks and feels luxurious. Cheap materials can make your jewelry look cheap as well.

2. Pay attention to details: Take the time to make sure your beads are strung evenly, your wire loops are tight, and your finishes are polished. Small details can make a big difference in the overall appearance of your jewelry.

3. Practice good design principles: Consider color, texture, and balance when creating your jewelry. Look for inspiration from magazines, online tutorials, and other sources to help you develop your design skills.

4. Keep it simple: Avoid using too many different types of beads or overly complicated designs. Clean lines and simple shapes can make a piece of jewelry look elegant and sophisticated.

5. Finish your work properly: Make sure that your jump rings are closed tightly, your crimp beads are secure, and your wire ends are properly trimmed. A professional-looking finish can make all the difference in the final product.

6. Take your time: Rushing through a project can result in mistakes and a sloppy-looking piece of jewelry. Take your time and work carefully to ensure that each component is crafted with care.

Remember, practice makes perfect when it comes to making jewelry. Don't be afraid to experiment and try new techniques, and be patient with yourself as you develop your skills. With time and dedication, you can create beautiful, professional-looking bead jewelry that you'll be proud to wear or give as gifts.

Section 3- Instructional Guide To Care For Your Bead Jewelry

Here are some tips for caring for your bead jewelry:

1. Store your jewelry properly: Keep your bead jewelry in a cool, dry place, away from direct sunlight and moisture. Avoid storing multiple pieces of jewelry in the same container, as they can scratch or tangle.

2. Clean your jewelry regularly: Use a soft, damp cloth to gently clean your jewelry. Avoid using harsh chemicals or abrasive materials, as they can damage your beads or metal components.

3. Remove your jewelry before swimming or showering: Chlorine and saltwater can damage your jewelry, as can exposure to water over time. To avoid damage, remove your jewelry before swimming or showering.

4. Avoid exposing your jewelry to heat or sunlight: Heat and sunlight can cause your jewelry to fade or warp. To protect your jewelry, store it in a cool, dry place and avoid leaving it in direct sunlight.

5. Be careful when handling your jewelry: Beads can be delicate and easily damaged if mishandled. When putting on or taking off your jewelry, be gentle to avoid accidentally pulling or twisting your beads.

By following these tips, you can help keep your bead jewelry looking beautiful for years to come. With proper care and maintenance, your jewelry can become a treasured part of your collection.

Chapter 7: Selling Your Bead Jewelry

Section 1- Tips For Selling Your Bead Jewelry

If you're interested in selling your bead jewelry, here are some tips to help you get started:

1. Define Your Style: Take some time to define your style and niche within the market. This will help you develop a unique brand and create jewelry that appeals to your target audience.

2. Build an Online Presence: Create an online presence to showcase your bead jewelry, whether it's through a website or social media platforms like Instagram or Facebook. Use high-quality images and descriptions to showcase your work and attract potential customers.

3. Attend Craft Shows and Markets: Attend local craft shows and markets to showcase your jewelry in person. This will allow customers to see and touch your jewelry, and provide an opportunity for you to connect with potential customers.

4. Consignment and Wholesale: Consider consignment or wholesale opportunities with local boutiques or online stores that specialize in handmade jewelry.

5. Offer Customization: Offering customization options can attract customers who are looking for personalized and unique jewelry. This can be as simple as offering different colors or lengths for your existing designs.

6. Build Relationships: Building relationships with your customers can lead to repeat business and positive word-of-mouth recommendations. Provide excellent customer service and follow up with customers to ensure their satisfaction.

Remember, selling your bead jewelry takes time and effort. Be patient and persistent, and keep experimenting and learning to improve your craft. With dedication and hard work, you can turn your love of bead jewelry making into a successful business.

Section 2- Setting Up An Online Store

If you're interested in setting up an online store to sell your bead jewelry, here are some steps to follow:

1. Choose a platform: There are many platforms available to create an online store, including Etsy, Shopify, and WooCommerce. Consider the features, fees, and ease of use when choosing a platform.

2. Create a name and branding: Choose a name for your store and create a consistent brand across all of your online and offline marketing materials. Use a professional logo and color scheme to create a cohesive look.

3. Create product listings: Create detailed product listings for each of your bead jewelry pieces, including high-quality images, descriptions, and pricing information.

4. Set up payment and shipping options: Choose payment options that are secure and easy to use, such as PayPal or credit card processing. Set up shipping options and rates that are competitive and affordable for your customers.

5. Market your store: Promote your online store through social media, email marketing, and other advertising channels. Consider offering special promotions or discounts to attract new customers.

6. Provide excellent customer service: Provide prompt responses to customer inquiries and feedback, and ensure that your products are shipped promptly and arrive in good condition.

Remember, setting up an online store takes time and effort. Be patient and persistent, and keep experimenting and learning to improve your store's performance. With dedication and hard work, you can turn your love of bead jewelry making into a successful online business.

Section 3- Marketing Your Jewelry

Marketing is an essential aspect of selling your bead jewelry, and there are several ways to promote your jewelry and reach potential customers:

1. Social media: Use social media platforms such as Instagram, Facebook, and Pinterest to showcase your bead jewelry pieces and connect with potential customers. Use high-quality images and engaging captions to promote your work and attract followers.

2. Craft shows and markets: Attend local craft shows and markets to showcase your jewelry in person. This will allow customers to see and touch your jewelry, and provide an opportunity for you to connect with potential customers.

3. Consignment and wholesale: Consider consignment or wholesale opportunities with local boutiques or online stores that specialize in handmade jewelry.

4. Email marketing: Build an email list of interested customers and send regular updates about new jewelry pieces, promotions, and events.

5. Collaborate with bloggers and influencers: Partner with bloggers and influencers in the jewelry or fashion industry to promote your work and reach a wider audience.

6. Offer giveaways and promotions: Offer giveaways and promotions to attract new customers and generate buzz around your brand.

Remember, marketing is an ongoing process, and it takes time and effort to build a loyal customer base. Be patient and persistent, and keep experimenting and learning to improve your marketing strategies. With dedication and hard work, you can turn your love of bead jewelry making into a successful business.

Chapter 8: Conclusion

Section 1- Summary Of Key Points

Sure, here's a summary of the key points covered in this book outline on bead jewelry making for beginners:

- Bead jewelry making involves using beads, wire, and other materials to create jewelry pieces.
- There are many types of beads available, including seed beads, glass beads, and crystal beads.
- Basic tools and materials needed for bead jewelry making include pliers, wire cutters, beads, and wire.
- Techniques for creating bead jewelry include stringing, using crimp beads, creating wire loops, knotting, and using jump rings.

- To create professional-looking jewelry, it's important to choose a design, sketch out your design, choose color schemes, and add embellishments.
- Advanced techniques for bead jewelry making include bead weaving and wire wrapping.
- To sell your bead jewelry, you can set up an online store, attend craft shows and markets, and use social media and email marketing to promote your work.
- Marketing your jewelry involves using a variety of strategies, including social media, email marketing, consignment and wholesale, collaborating with bloggers and influencers, and offering giveaways and promotions.

These are just a few of the key points covered in this book outline, but they should give you a good starting point if you're interested in learning more about bead jewelry making for beginners.

Section 2- Inspiration For Future Bead Jewelry Projects

Here are some ideas for future bead jewelry projects:

1. Statement necklaces: Experiment with different color schemes and bead combinations to create bold and unique necklaces that make a statement.

2. Layered bracelets: Combine different types of beads and materials to create layered bracelets that can be worn individually or stacked for a bohemian look.

3. Wire wrapped rings: Learn the art of wire wrapping and create delicate and intricate rings using colorful beads.

4. Beaded tassel earrings: Add a fun and playful touch to your jewelry collection with beaded tassel earrings in bright and bold colors.

5. Mixed media necklaces: Combine beads with other materials such as leather, cord, or fabric to create mixed media necklaces that are both unique and versatile.

6. Bridal jewelry: Use crystals, pearls, and other elegant materials to create beautiful and sophisticated bridal jewelry pieces.

7. Beaded cuffs: Create bold and edgy cuffs using chunky beads and wire, perfect for adding a statement to any outfit.

Remember to always experiment and have fun with your bead jewelry projects, and don't be afraid to try new techniques and materials to create truly unique and personalized pieces.

Section 3- Final Thoughts And Encouragement For Continuing To Create Beautiful Bead Jewelry

Bead jewelry making is a fun and rewarding hobby that allows you to express your creativity and create unique and personalized pieces of jewelry. While it may seem intimidating at first, with practice and patience, you can learn the skills needed to create beautiful and professional-looking jewelry.

Remember to take your time and enjoy the process, experiment with different techniques and materials, and don't be afraid to make mistakes. Each mistake provides an ample opportunity to learn as well as improve your skills.

Bead jewelry making can also be a great way to connect with others who share your passion. Joining a local bead club or taking a class can provide you with the opportunity to learn new techniques, exchange ideas, and make new friends.

So keep creating, keep learning, and most importantly, have fun! With dedication and practice, you can create beautiful and unique bead jewelry pieces that you'll be proud to wear and share with others.

Made in the USA
Columbia, SC
28 December 2025

77029662R00050